The Trustworthy Confidant

The Trustworthy Confidant

Table Of Contents

Foreword

Self-confidence starts within you.

Your assessment of your self-worth is what determines your self-confidence. Somehow, there is gap between what you are now in your life and what you want to become in the future.

The larger the gap between your self-image and your ideal self, the lesser is the level of your self-confidence. Get all the info you need here.

The Confidence

Confidant – Your Trusted Guide To Building Confidence And Succeeding In Anything

Chapter 1:

Introduction

Synopsis

When you have high self-confidence, you are able to take risks and face new challenges with an open mind that you can achieve what your personal goals are.

You believe in yourself that you will succeed and that you can make things happen. This allows you to do things that will direct you reaching your dreams and being the person you want to become.

The Advantages

On the other hand, when you have low self-confidence, you are afraid of taking risks and this disables you to grab opportunities that will help you achieve things in your life. You are doubtful with your skills and capabilities and your mind is filled with negative thoughts.

Hence, even if you desire to be a better person in the future with a lot of achievements, you cannot take a step to reach that stage in your life. You are getting coward of realizing your visions.

Being highly confident and over confident are two different things you must know for you to be guided. High-confidence enables you do things right for your success. It will enhance your performance in whatever tasks you encounter. However, being too much confident will lead you to frustrations. Why? Because when you are too much confident, you neglect the simple things to prepare in pursuit of your success. You are thinking you can do everything, and when you are not able to do it, you will find yourself grieving too much for your loss.

Perhaps there are aspects in your life that contribute to your current level of self-confidence. Well, self-confidence is really founded in your belief in yourself. However, the people around you can also affect your upbringing as a person.

One of the most influential people in young people's lives is their parents. Yes, parents know best for their children. Definitely they should be the first persons who will help youth to build confidence within them and seek to achieve things for their future.

Yet, we have to admit, not all parents are applying what they know is best for their children. It is sad to note that parents are abusing their children, battered them, shout at them often and give them a sense of unimportance. Hence, youth with this kind of family would fell they are not needed, that they don't belong and that they do not have worth at all.

Other people who greatly affect young people's level confidence are their peers. Young as they are, they would want to belong in group of friends whom they can share their thoughts and problems. They seek to be with their peers whom they can be who and what they really are. If the youngsters do not belong in any peer group and stays on their own, they will feel that nobody like them. They will feel that they are unwanted and that they have no people to get along with. As a result, their self-confidence rockets down and becomes low.

How about you? What level are you in? Awareness of your strengths and weakness as well as you're your ability to achieve things will help you to understand what you are now as a person. As you further read this book, you will know how you can succeed in life with building high level of self-confidence.

Chapter 2:

Synopsis

Is self-confidence, born or made?

It can be both. Some people are born naturally with confidence. Others also acquired self-confidence as they seek to learn and understand it. Hence, they are the ones who made themselves confident.

Building

You too have the hope of becoming highly confident and find for yourself a higher ground to achieve success. You just have to be open to accept new knowledge and learn it.

Basically, you must understand how important self-confidence is in your life. With no second thoughts, high level of confidence is definitely very important because it defines how much you can be able to achieve in your life. Also, it contributes to your happiness as it impacts the ideal "you" you are eager to become. When you have knowledge I this importance, you will develop to have self-confidence that will drive you to be a successful person in whatever endeavor you have.

Self-confidence develops your ability to influence other people around you. The fact is that you cannot take a hold of any leadership role unless you have confidence in yourself. A leader has the ability to influence others to follow and convince them in your ideas. Without self-confidence, you yourself will be the first one to doubt your abilities.

This will affect the way you lead your subordinates. As research has shown, people are most likely to disapprove an idea from someone who proposes the plan is nervous at the time of proposal. Moreover, they will not trust you as well since even you don't trust yourself. If you are confident enough, you can sell your ideas effectively to them and they will have a confidence in you as their leader.

Perhaps, the best time to start building confidence is during a person's childhood. You can help children acquire confidence as they are yet much more flexible in accepting new knowledge and suggestions.

Children will low level of self-confidence are those who have poor performance in school. They do not participate in activities that much and most of the time spent a day alone in the corner of the classroom. Somehow, you can teach them how to overcome the attitude of being shy and non-participative.

Children as they are, defending themselves of things they don't want to do is yet a difficult thing for them to do. Normally in school, children are forced by their parents to join extra-curricular activities which they might not be happy joining at. Then, when they fail to perform it, a portion of their confidence is taken away by that activity.

You can make a change in the lives of these children. They are very vulnerable to low self-confidence and you can contribute to bring success in their lives. A good foundation of building self-confidence is when they are yet in their childhood phase.

Chapter 3:

How to Conquer Fear in Any Situation

Synopsis

Are your fears taking the most out of your life? You don't need to suffer from all these fears. You can overcome them.

Fear is something you cannot take away. However, you can do something to lessen the pain it will cause you. This is not about your fear of heights, snakes, darkness, water, or any like.

Only the doctors and psychiatrist can give you the solution to those fears. The focuses of this are your fears towards reaching for your goal of succeeding in your life.

Are you afraid of talking to people? Are you afraid of getting mistakes? Somehow, these are some of our fears that will hinder us from accomplishing things we want to achieve.

How To

You can conquer you fear in any situation you are in. First, you must have a clear understanding of what your fear is all about. What causes it should be known by you for you to be able to do appropriate things to overcome it. When you have full understanding of your fear, it would be easier for you to make the necessary adjustments to conquer it in time.

As soon as you have known your fear already, you must have the courage to face it. Facing your fears is the only access to overcoming it. You cannot spend the rest of your life avoiding your fear. You cannot hide from it. You cannot go away from it.

The only thing you can do is face it. By then, you will know how to surpass it ahead.

When you get to face your fears, get exposed to it. Or it can be the other way around; allow your fears to penetrate and get exposed to you. As you get exposed to your fears, you will find it easy to go through it. Have an ample dosage of it and see for yourself how you can make things happen.

While you are exposing yourself in your fear, trust that someone will deliver you from it. There is a Supreme Being that can help you along the way. Trust in His providence. He is under control and He can give you the wisdom you need to overcome life's fears and obstacles. Change your perspective.

Somehow, a positive outlook in life will help you get through your fear and overcome it. Whatever negative things that happen in your life, there is still a future that awaits you. Focus on the positive things and underplay the negative thoughts within you.

Finally, don't linger on the past. Instead, fix your eyes on the present and the future that is waiting ahead of you. Set your mind in the prize you want to achieve in this life, the prize of reaching the success peak.

Chapter 4:

Synopsis

The art of public speaking is not just about merely delivering those long speeches. It is about conquering every struggle you encounter as you seek to express your thoughts and ideas to a large number of audiences listening. The quality of your speaking matters most. And this is where you should be able to learn more.

The Art

The best way to deliver your speech is having a relaxed mind and body. Butterflies may be flying all around your stomach, but manage yourself. Get a breath of fresh air and see the importance of being relaxed all throughout your speech.

Your knees might be trembling, your voice might be shaky, your mouth might be about to dry up. So, just relax. Take it easy. Don't think that it will be your greatest downfall. Instead think of it as an avenue for you to better the lives of the people who will be listening to you in a few minutes.

Get a little nervous. Being overconfident is a must avoid. Sometimes, the worst frustration comes from a person who thinks everything can be done in no sweat. In a way, that nervous feeling you have can help get the adrenaline to get through the challenge of public speaking.

Think about a scenario of your house burning. Because of your nervousness, you were able to carry your refrigerator alone. Amazing, right? It happens to a lot of people.

Adrenaline rush can help you get things done. Same is true with public speaking. You can do it with that little dose of nervousness you have. So, exploit it. You can do it well while in the state of being nervous.

Never attempt to achieve perfection. Let yourself be human. Nobody is perfect; the same hold true for you. No public speaking is perfect. Definitely, nobody in the audience expect perfection from you. Simply aim to express yourself to the people around.

They want to hear your experiences, your advices and your life insights. Inspire them with what you say. In the end, that is what they need- inspiration to live life at its best. Never try to impress them by being perfect because that is something impossible.

Develop a positive pressure. Yes, pressure can be useful as you deliver your speech. However, you must be able to control the pressure in such a way that it gets you better in speaking. Some people get pressured and they fail.

Some also gets pressured and succeed. Choose you side. Get pressured to deliver the speech well and not the kind of pressure that will leave you afraid of taking the risk.

Practice it well. Practicing has always been such a very effective tool for you to deliver your speech. Well, you can employ all those tools, techniques and methods you have learned from the professionals.

But, practicing your own way and style is still way off better. As you get to practice your speech, you get used to it and familiarize every detail of it.

Hence, it will be an easier task for you to deliver it in front of the people. Most people would suggest that you practice it the night before your actual speech. By that, you will be able to see what things are yet lacking in your speech and you will be able to work on it still.

Lastly, visualize how your speech will look like. With that, you can be guided of the progress of your speech.
As the day comes for you to finally deliver your speech, relax and be yourself. Be optimistic. Believe in yourself. Always think you can do it.

Chapter 5:

Synopsis

Break Walls, Build Bridges

Sometimes, we get so engrossed with ourselves that we are unknowingly building walls around us. It seems we do not want to be interrupted, interfered and disrupted.

We find our own selves a home of refuge and comfort that we tend to exclude others from it..

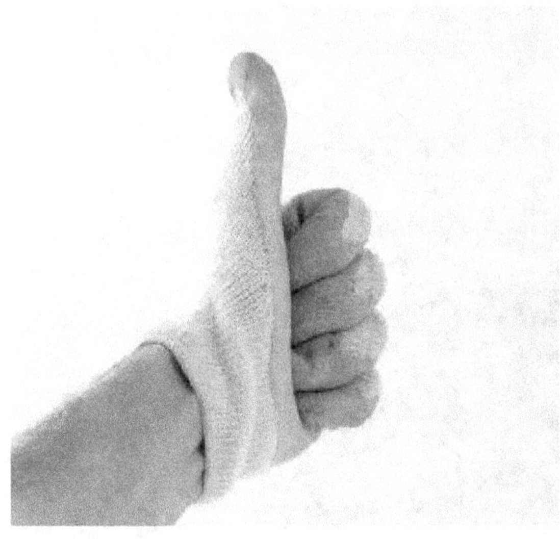

Approaching People

However, in approaching people, the wall we build is not anymore a protection. Instead, it is a barrier that hinders us from connecting to people around us. Approaching people is leaving your comfort zone to connect with people.

So, why keep those walls? Break it and get through. You will never know how it is like to meet new people and learn from them unless you break those walls.

Anyhow, you can replace those walls with bridges. Bridges are avenues where you can cross and reach out to others. Share your life with them and learn from them as well. Bridges are what you need to get connected. Build those bridges and approach people with confidence.

Develop a Friendly Mind

The power of your mind greatly affects how you interact with the people around. Everything we feel and experience is because of the way our mind thinks and how we perceive the situations we encounter.

If we think a problem is very difficult to solve, it would really be hard for you to find solutions for it. If you think you are not as good as others, your insecurity will take its toll on you. That is how powerful your mind can be.

Same is true for the way you mingle with other people. Their conduct, manners and attitudes may be acceptable to you or not depending on the way you think of these aspects. You can think of hating them, and you really will. But if you think of liking them, you will definitely find yourself getting along with them well.

So, develop a friendly perception. See things on the brighter side.

Be exciting

Don't get yourself too overwhelmed on something that you keep on sharing that subject to the people around you. Be observant in their responses and get to know if they are still interested with what you are talking about or if they are still listening to you. Don't bore them with the same subject in the whole duration of your conversation. Keep them excited, don't get them bored.

Listen more, Talk less

Most of us want to talk more and share to others our feelings and anything under the sun. However, talking more will only show them you only want yourself to be talked about. Get interested in their lives. Listen to their thoughts.

Give them the chance to be talked about. As much as you want to be given attention, show them your eagerness to be a part of their lives. Never focus on yourself. Be sensitive to them. Get yourself curious with what are happening in them as well.

Limit your questions

Asking questions is an effective tool to show you are curious about other people's lives. However, throwing a lot of questions to them will give them a wrong signal on you. Don't think of yourself as an investigator or an examiner that you will ask everything and even anything about them. Know how to shift from asking into making a statement. Balance your conversation.

Be yourself

Perhaps, this is the best advice for you. Whatever you are engaged into whether you are conversing with people or performing tasks, always wear the real you. Don't think that it would be better if you will be the person they want you to become.

Instead, show them how you value yourself and how you seek to approach them in the most natural way of being yourself. You don't need to buy expensive clothes to fit in, or wear beautiful makeup if you are not used to it. Being you is still the best way to approach people with no fear.

Chapter 6:
Instant Confidence Boosters

Synopsis

"Let's cross the bridge when we get there."

This saying is perhaps most people's excuses before they get to realize the importance of having self-confidence.

Change is inevitable. Change is constant. It happens to everything. It happens to everyone. However, the issue lies in the time we think it is right for us to change.

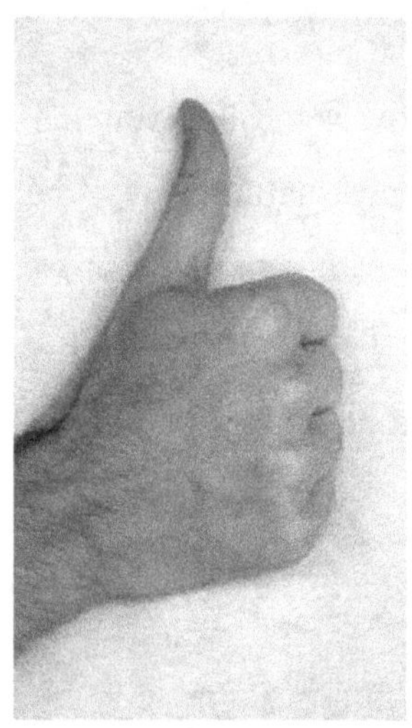

Boosts

Imagine yourself in one scenario with a glass of water. You were given a glass with hot water in it. When you were told to hold it, you immediately released because the pain was not bearable.

Now, imagine yourself holding a glass, gradually poured with hot water in it. At first, you are still holding the glass because the water is not yet full and its heat is still bearable. Soon, the glass was filled with hot water and all you can do was to lose your grip off that glass. Why did you not release it immediately? Because you thought you can bear it long. You held it tight, not until the heat was getting worse.

What is common among the two examples?

Most of us would only consider the idea of change when we cannot anymore endure the pain of holding something in us. And definitely, that is how we treat our lack of self-confidence.

The fact is that, lack of self-confidence will not hurt us right away. How good it might be if lack of confidence operates in our lives just like the first example above- that when we lack it, we will immediately feel the pain of it and would release it immediately because it is giving us too much pain.

It is sad to note that the lack of self-confidence is like the second example. We thought its fine. We thought we can bear it. We thought we can endure it. But the pain will be experienced gradually. Until we realize the pain is enough for us to let go of and shift to another perspective, we will never lose our grip of it.

Perhaps, we consider unlocking our confidence when we are left with no more options. When the world is already crashing us and destructing us, that is the time when we unlock our confidence. We treat it as last resort to our problem, when in fact lack of self-confidence itself is the problem we need to solve.

All of us will definitely have our own turning-points in our lives. Time will come when we will finally see the importance of boosting the confidence within us.

Yet, the best time is now.

When will you think of developing high level of confidence?

When all opportunities around are already gone?

When you are already old and cannot exploit it any longer?

When you are about to die?

Do you think that is the time?

Definitely it's not. In fact it would be too late if that's the case.

Decide on things wisely. Now is not yet too late for you to change your life. You can make things happen if only you understand how confidence can be helpful to you.

The word "confidence" may not be pleasing and appealing to us, but when we are able to experience it, we will see how wonderful and productive it is to bring confidence wherever we are.

I would not probably be an easy task. But you will absolutely learn it and appreciate it along the way.

Wrapping Up

People who have experienced failures in their lives think that they are born twinned with all the problems in the world. They are hopeless. They think it's the end of this world. They think nothing good will happen to them.

Perhaps, you too think of these things.

But you don't have any reasons t pursue those thoughts in your mind. Rather, you have all the reasons to think that you can make a difference in your life.

Yes, you absolutely can.

The key is simply within you. Your confidence is the key. You just have to unlock it to see it work for you. The eagerness and willingness within you to employ this key is a must. In the end, nobody can execute it, except you.

These are the things you need to remember:

You have worth

How do you see yourself? Do you see yourself as someone who has the ability and the skills to change your life? Do you think you can be influential to others and lead towards achieving their personal goals? Do you view yourself as someone who doesn't have worth at all? Do you have what it takes be successful in the future?

How you see yourself determines what you can achieve. You may be a man with no wealth and success now, but as long as see yourself as someone you has worth, you will find for yourself ways to change the way your life works.

Plan ahead

Planning involves defining goals and objectives ahead of time. You can be successful if as early as now, you are already clear with the goals you want to achieve. Your personal goals will guide you of what actions should be taken to step forward, each step going farther from you and nearer to the peak of success.

A man with no goals is the same as playing basketball with no chances of winning. Why? Simply because shooting the ball in the goal is the basis for earning points and winning. The same holds true in achieving success in life. You actions will be credited to your goal. Indeed, you must have a goal in order to win life's battles and struggles.

Set Examples

A lot of people in this world has been there and has done that. Those people can be your role models in achieving your goals. Their experiences will give you insights in how you will realize your dreams in life. They are the people whom you can follow. Learn from them and work hard to be just like them- successful.

Have the right confidence

Being over confident is not the right confidence. Over-confidence is not helpful. In fact, it is dangerous. Dangerous in such a way that it will mislead you to the things you are capable of. When you are over confident, you think you can do everything and that you will succeed in every undertaking. However, this world doesn't provide you with an all-success story. There are ups and downs- and you have to understand that failures happen. People with over confidence easily get frustrated when they fail.

All you need is high level of self-confidence. No more, no less. Just the exact amount and you can be flexible in whatever circumstances in life you encounter.

Be true to yourself

We are all created unique and distinct from each other. We have our own skills, talents and abilities. We have different attitudes, beliefs and perspectives.

You don't need to be just like the other people to achieve success. All you have to do is believe in yourself, accept whoever you are and trust that you will be able to do great things and achieve huge success.
Just be true to yourself.